4000 DAYS

BY PETER QUILTER

SERVING THEATRE

S F

SINCE 1830

WWW.SAMUELFRENCH.CO.UK
WWW.SAMUELFRENCH.COM

FOR AMATEUR PRODUCTION ENQUIRIES

UNITED KINGDOM AND WORLD EXCLUDING NORTH AMERICA
plays@SamuelFrench-London.co.uk
020 7255 4302/01
UNITED STATES AND CANADA
info@SamuelFrench.com
1-866-598-8449
Each title is subject to availability from Samuel French, depending upon country of performance.

4000 Days was first performed at Park Theatre, London,
on 14 January 2016 with the following cast:

Michael	**Alistair McGowan**
Carol	**Maggie Ollerenshaw**
Paul	**Daniel Weyman**

Director	**Matt Aston**
Designer	**Rebecca Brower**
Lighting Designer	**Tom Boucher**
Sound Designer	**Damian Coldwell**
Video Designer	**Alexander Thomas**
Casting	**Jenkins McShane Casting**

Producer	**Douglas McJannet for Covent Garden Productions Ltd**
Producer	**Sam Julyan for Covent Garden Productions Ltd**
Production Manager	**Heather Doole**
Costume Supervisor	**Molly Syrett**
Stage Manager	**Catherine Cooper**
Assistant Stage Manager	**Jack Dormer**

In association with Park Theatre

Author's Note

The inspiration for this play came from a dream I had. This is unique for me. But the fact is that one night I dreamed that I had a pile of newspapers by my bed and I had to work through each of them, day by day. For some reason, a chunk of my life, or a piece of my memory, had disappeared. So I had to read the papers to catch up on everything I'd missed.

I developed this idea into the play *4000 Days* after discovering that people who suffer comas sometimes wake up with memory loss. Adults believe they are still teenagers, mothers don't recognize their own children, people feel that the last decade has simply just not existed. I thought it was a good set up for a piece of theatre and this dramatic, funny, dream-like idea had its world premiere at London's Park Theatre in 2016.

As this author's note is being written in advance of the premiere, I am unable to share any informed thoughts on how productions might handle the various aspects of the play and characters. But in a way, this is a good thing as it gives you a clean slate and you can discover the staging of the play for yourselves.

However, I do have some technical suggestions. Firstly, you will read that the play has the option of using a couple of video sequences. Both take place during blackouts, so a screen can be brought into view for these sequences or it can be positioned permanently above or to the side of the stage. Walls of the set itself might even be used to show projections. Companies will create their own videos for the show, using material gathered from online video website sources such as Youtube. But in the event that these video sequences are just too complicated or expensive for you to achieve, the show can play perfectly well without them. The show would just move from the blackout into the next scene. So I don't mind if you want to skip them completely. But I encourage you to use the video sequences if you possibly can as they will add a very nice extra touch to the show. It's up to you.

Another technical aspect of the staging is a mural that is painted on the hospital wall. This mural is gradually painted during the course of the show and so grows each time we see it. Clever designers might come up with a brilliant alternative way of doing this. But my suggestion is this – that the back wall of the set is made up of separate blank panels. Each panel has a section of the mural painted on the back. So as the play progresses, each panel is turned around to face the audience, and part of the mural is revealed. This is not particularly complicated to achieve, so please don't be frightened off by the thought of it. It's a potentially beautiful visual element to the show and I'm sure you'll be able to make it work with a simple bit of carpentry and some artistic flair.

Beyond these technical aspects, I really think this is a play that will stand or fall on the strength of the actors. There are three strong and equal roles here so make the best of them. If cast well, and intelligently directed, the show will be both emotional and entertaining.

Well, that's my dream anyway...

Peter Quilter
2016

CHARACTERS

CAROL – Michael's mother, 60's/70's. Waspish and difficult, with a dry sense of humour. Hides her deep feelings behind a cool veneer.

PAUL – In his 40's/50's. A pleasant gay man with a good heart, but perhaps a little ordinary and lacking in passion.

MICHAEL – Carol's son, 40's/50's. Charming and artistic, with natural wit and intelligence.

The age of the characters is flexible. Michael and Paul can be in their 30's, 40's or 50's. Carol can be in her 50's, 60's or 70's, depending on the age of Michael

There is a brief non-speaking cameo at the end of the show – this role should be taken by one of the Stage Management Team or an understudy

SETTING

Modern day. A large private room in a private hospital. The back wall of the room is vast and beige. A large bed surrounded by heart monitoring machines, brain monitoring machines, a drip, charts and instructions on various clipboards. Cards, flowers, bottles of water, etc. One large armchair stage right by the window, plus a simple plastic chair stage left by the door. Michael occupies the bed. He is in a coma. A music player is prominent in the room and set up to play his favourite music.

Twice during the show there are video sequences, requiring some kind of video screen to descend.

During Act Two, the back wall of the room will gradually display a giant painted mural. The simplest way of achieving this is to have the back wall made of three or four separate panels with the mural painted on the hidden other side. These panels can then be quickly turned around to reveal the artwork at the appropriate time.

ACT ONE

Scene One

Music: Remember *(NILSSON)* – Sung by Harry Nilsson

Lights slowly rise on the hospital room as the song plays.

*CAROL enters, carrying a large bunch of fresh flowers. She puts the flowers in a vase. She kisses **MICHAEL**, who does not respond. She holds his hand for a moment and then she settles into the armchair and reads a book.*

*PAUL enters a little while after this and they briefly but coldly acknowledge each other. **PAUL** has also brought fresh flowers, a smaller bunch, plus some sandwiches in a brown paper bag. The music cross-fades from the auditorium to the music player on stage. **PAUL** turns the music off.*

CAROL I also brought flowers.

PAUL Yes, I see. I'll get another vase.

CAROL There's nowhere to put yours, really.

PAUL I'll get another vase.

He heads out of the door, pausing for a moment to look back.

…Anything?

CAROL No. But he looks very peaceful today. …Why don't you leave those? The nurse will be in soon, she'll find something to put them in. A smaller vase.

PAUL *puts the flowers down on the bed and sits on the plastic chair next to the bed.*

PAUL I asked for Doctor Medina, but he's not in today.

CAROL Apparently, he's gone to a funeral. Let's hope it's not for one of his patients…

She puts a cigarette in her mouth.

PAUL You're not smoking?

CAROL As you said, his doctor's not here today.

PAUL What's that got to do with anything?

CAROL Michael won't mind. He's been breathing in my cigarettes since he was a baby. In the womb, in fact. The books say we should surround him with familiar smells.

PAUL Perfumed candles, not Marlboro Lights. I'd prefer we didn't give him cancer while he was sleeping.

CAROL I should have thought cancer was the least of his concerns right now. I'll stand by the window if it bothers you that much.

PAUL It's not *me* I'm thinking about. It's never me I'm thinking about.

CAROL *reluctantly goes to the window and smokes her cigarette.*

CAROL He had some friends come to visit, but as I wasn't here, they couldn't let them in. Mark somebody and another chap. They left a card.

PAUL *locates and reads the card.*

…They enclosed a little pin drive with music on it as well. I put it on to play. Not sure if it's what he likes.

PAUL Mark knows what he likes.

CAROL Does he? I've never heard of him. Certainly never seen him before. It's strange seeing all these cards from people I just don't know at all. He had this whole other life. I don't even know if they're decent. Are his friends decent?

PAUL No, some of them are totally *in*-decent. I'm not a fan of many of them. But there are others, a few that are – you know, genuinely nice. That genuinely love him.

CAROL Oh yes, he's always loved. Never been a shortage of that. It's his charm. *(a long drag of the cigarette)* ...He gets that from me.

A smile from CAROL. PAUL *leans over to* MICHAEL, *touches his hair, looks in his eyes. Talks to him.*

PAUL ...Michael... ...Michael...

He takes MICHAEL*'s hand and sits back in the chair.*

CAROL ...You should have brought a book. It gets very boring just sat there holding his hand. Plus I started to get cramp. Not that I'm complaining.

PAUL I don't have long. They only give me an hour for lunch.

Using his other hand, he takes a packet of sandwiches out of his brown paper bag.

CAROL You'll have trouble eating those if you don't let go of his hand.

PAUL I can't let go.

CAROL ...We may have to.

PAUL looks at CAROL *sternly.*

PAUL I don't believe that. Not at all.

CAROL I don't either. But you have to at least acknowledge the possibility.

PAUL Why?

CAROL Because, Paul – things don't always go as you hope, in this life. You'll learn that as you get older. And sometimes it's better to face things in advance. Just in case. Otherwise the shock can kill you. And suddenly there are *two* bodies on the floor. I'm not pessimistic. It's just damage control.

PAUL And Michael gets his charm from you, you said?

CAROL I know I'm not charming. *(a last puff on her cigarette)* But I'm not dull either.

She throws her cigarette out of the window.

PAUL Don't do that – you could set some pensioner's hair on fire.

CAROL *(laughing, amused by this)* I never thought of that!

She looks excitedly out of the window. Then back at **PAUL,** *who is holding* **MICHAEL** *'s hand with one hand and struggling to open his sandwiches with the other.*

…Oh for goodness sake, I'll hold his hand and you eat your sandwiches.

She crosses to stage left.

…Come on.

PAUL *agrees and gently lets go of* **MICHAEL** *'s hand.* **CAROL** *sits in the plastic chair and holds* **MICHAEL** *'s hand.*

PAUL *crosses to the armchair and eats his sandwiches.*

…You should try the canteen. Have lunch in the canteen.

PAUL Is the food good?

CAROL Don't be ridiculous. But at least you get a hot meal.

time she arrived, everything was tidy, disinfected and gleaming. It was completely pointless paying her the money. They do pass judgement on you, cleaners. They don't say anything. But they spend the whole morning looking at your dirty shelves and disapproving. ...But the place is clean?

PAUL Very.

CAROL Good. *(to* **MICHAEL***)* ...You hear that, Michael my darling?

She strokes his hair.

PAUL ...Do you want half of this sandwich? I've lost my appetite.

CAROL What's in it?

PAUL Cheese and salad.

CAROL *(laughing)* You really do push the boat out, don't you. ...No, I'll get something from the canteen. It may not be disgusting today. We live in hope – don't we?

PAUL Yes. We do.

CAROL *lets go of* **MICHAEL***'s hand.*

CAROL ...So you're staying here tonight?

PAUL Yes.

CAROL ...I don't know. May be it should be me. *(taking hold of his hand again)* What if he wakes up?

PAUL If he wakes up, I'll be here.

CAROL Yes, but he'll want to see his mother's face first, won't he.

PAUL Why?

CAROL *(confused)* What do you mean, 'why?'

PAUL He just wants to see somebody he loves.

CAROL *(a little laugh)* …There's no greater love than that between a mother and a son. I don't expect you to understand.

PAUL I understand he only visits you once every three months.

CAROL We're not so insecure that we need to be in each other's pockets. I don't think he has ever wanted someone who keeps him on a tight leash.

PAUL That's not our relationship.

CAROL You never give him any space. That is true – don't deny it. You seem to control everything. He always looks so emotionally drained. No wonder he only gets to visit me every twelve weeks, the poor boy is exhausted.

PAUL You don't know anything.

CAROL I know a great deal. He tells me every detail.

PAUL No he doesn't. He keeps as much information from you as he can. Doesn't want to give you any ammunition. You store stuff up. So that when you want to get really nasty you have a few bullets at your finger tips. That's who *you* are – and it's not very attractive, is it. No wonder it took a *coma* to get us in a room together.

Silence for a moment. **PAUL** *stands up.*

…I want to sit back next to him.

CAROL I'm here now. Wait your turn.

PAUL Don't be childish. I have to get back to work soon.

CAROL So you keep saying. The washing powder needs you!

PAUL What did I ever actually do to piss you off so much?

CAROL That's quite a question. Do I have time to make a list?

PAUL I realize you had other ideas for Michael, but just remember that –

CAROL No – that's not correct. He made his own choices and that's just fine. You don't plan your children's futures. Not unless you want to get hurt. But we mothers do reserve the right to be very disappointed.

PAUL I'm sorry you feel that way.

CAROL Yes, me too. But it doesn't matter, does it. We don't have to like each other, do we? There's no law insists on it. As long as Michael likes you, that's what counts… I suppose. Though I'm not completely sure. It's funny, you being so devoted to him during all this. From what I hear, the two of you never stopped arguing.

PAUL We have strong opinions on things, so yes. I think it's healthy for a relationship. Anyway two men together is more complicated. Men and women tend to look at a problem differently. Two guys – well, you just go round in circles. But a lot of couples argue, Carol. It doesn't mean they don't love each other.

CAROL I never argued with my husbands. I found it much better to stand there silently while they rattled off all their fury. Then when they became exhausted by my lack of response – we went to bed. Works wonderfully.

PAUL You don't seem to be able to be silent with me very often.

CAROL I'm not married to you. Different game, different rules.

PAUL Then I'd rather, when this is over, that we can simply go back to avoiding each other again.

CAROL I don't avoid anybody. I much prefer to look them in the eye. See what they're made of. Presuming they're made of anything at all.

PAUL Let me have the chair.

CAROL I said *no*. Finish your sandwich.

> **PAUL** *crosses to the bed and defiantly lays on it, next to* **MICHAEL**. **CAROL** *is furious.*

> Get off the bed! *(standing)* You can't be on the bed! The wires – the drip!

PAUL Oh relax. I lay here all the time.

CAROL You shouldn't! Paul!

PAUL I'm not moving. I'm not moving till I go to work. *(looks at his watch)* I've got ten minutes.

CAROL Paul! I mean it now.

PAUL Go and get a drink or something. Come back in ten minutes.

CAROL I'm not leaving.

PAUL Then shut up and put some music on.

CAROL Don't you – …Nobody *ever* talks to me like that.

PAUL Oh, of course they do. That's what gets your battery started in the morning.

> **CAROL** *fumes for a moment, then looks at her watch.*

CAROL Five minutes – that's all. Then I set the sheets on fire.

> *Realising she's done with the argument, she strides over to the armchair and slumps into it.*

> And if you dislodge any of those wires, I'll have you killed. Do you hear me?

> **PAUL** *turns on the music player via a nearby remote control. It plays –*

In The Wee Small Hours Of The Morning
(MANN/HILLIARD) – Sung by Frank Sinatra

Noticing the remaining portion of **PAUL***'s sandwich,*
CAROL *picks it up and starts to eat it.* **PAUL** *snuggles
up to* **MICHAEL***. And the lights fade to blackout. The
music cross-fades from the player to the auditorium.*

Scene Two

The music continues. Lights rise dimly on the room.
It is night time. **PAUL** *is asleep in the armchair. He is*
wearing his underclothes, plus is covered in a blanket
or a dressing gown. Nothing happens for a while. Then,
and subtly at first, we detect movement from **MICHAEL**
in the bed. Eventually he starts to move more forcefully.

One sudden strong turn causes one of the wires or
tubes to come free and this sets off a red flashing light
in the room. The light wakes **PAUL***, who observes what*
is happening and rushes to the bed. He re-attaches the
wires/tubes as best he can. Over the music, we hear him
yell –

PAUL *(calling out)* Nurse! Nurse! *(he grabs hold of* **MICHAEL***)*
Michael! Michael!

The lights fade again to blackout.

CAROL Well… It doesn't matter because yesterday you woke up. You came out of the coma – it was a miracle. And they think now you'll be fine. Just fine. Of course, the issues with the 'blood clotting' still have to be dealt with – you won't be running a marathon any time soon. But – you're here. You came through. So that's what happened, Michael. Not with the medical bells and whistles, but the essential parts of the story. And it has a happy ending. And I love you so much.

She carefully embraces him.

MICHAEL A coma? That's quite scary.

CAROL You looked very content. And you were never alone. I was here. Or Paul was here – all day, all night. Paul was here when you first started to wake. He didn't leave this room all night or all of yesterday. You were very disorientated, I expect you weren't even aware he was here at all. He looked a complete wreck by last night, so the Doctor absolutely insisted he went home to get some sleep. He'll be back at noon or thereabouts. He'll be thrilled that you've woken today with a voice and all your marbles.

MICHAEL I hope so. I haven't checked down there yet.

A glance under the sheets and a cheeky smile. **CAROL** *laughs.*

CAROL Do you have any questions? Anything you need to know? Something I've missed out?

MICHAEL Only that you haven't told me who Paul is.

CAROL What do you mean?

MICHAEL Paul. The guy you say stayed all yesterday. I mean, I remember someone being here – but I thought he was the nurse. So – 'Paul' is a friend of yours?

CAROL I'm confused.

MICHAEL No, *I'm* confused, dear. I've been in a coma.

CAROL I don't understand if you're joking. I mean – it's not that funny. I'm sure Paul wouldn't find it funny, would he?

MICHAEL I've no idea. I don't know who he is.

CAROL Paul.

MICHAEL Yes.

CAROL *(insistent)* Paul.

MICHAEL I give up. It doesn't matter.

CAROL Michael –

MICHAEL It doesn't. Whatever. I was only asking who the man was, it can't be that important. Give me more coffee.

> **CAROL** *gives him the coffee.*

CAROL So…

MICHAEL What?

CAROL You *really* don't know who Paul is?

MICHAEL No, Mum. And I won't till you bloody tell me, will I. *(drinks the coffee)* This coffee's cold.

CAROL Michael – look at me. *(he does so)* Seriously now – are you joking?

> **MICHAEL** *holds his wires and tubes on display.*

MICHAEL Do I look like I'm joking?

> **CAROL** *locates a photo of* **MICHAEL** *and* **PAUL** *together which had been placed by the window with various other portraits of family and friends. She gives the photo to* **MICHAEL**.

CAROL This is him.

MICHAEL *examines the photo.*

MICHAEL Okay. …That's strange… I don't remember this picture. I look fucking terrible. When was this? I don't know this other guy – honestly.

CAROL Something's not right. I'm calling the Doctor back. I think you may have concussion or something. Post Comatic Stress Disorder.

MICHAEL You just made that up! There's no such thing.

CAROL Well I don't know! *(suddenly an idea)* How many fingers am I holding up?

She stands and holds up eight fingers.

MICHAEL Don't be ridiculous.

CAROL That's not answering the question.

MICHAEL I am not deranged just because I can't remember some guy in a boring suit.

CAROL I'm going to get somebody.

> **CAROL** *goes to the door and exits. But she returns just a few seconds later.*

…Who is the Prime Minister?

MICHAEL Who cares, they're all fascists.

CAROL Michael! – What year is it?

MICHAEL If you don't stop this – I'm going back to sleep for another three weeks.

CAROL Please. Answer the question. What year is it?

> **MICHAEL** *lets out a breath of exasperation.*

MICHAEL 2005. And get me a coffee.

CAROL Seriously, Michael.

MICHAEL Yes, seriously – with two sugars. I don't care what the nurses say.

CAROL *(angry, raising her voice)* Michael – What year is it?!

MICHAEL 2005! I told you. Why are you shouting?

> **CAROL** *puts her hand to her mouth as though in shock.*

…What's the matter?

CAROL That was – …That was *eleven* years ago.

MICHAEL What was?

CAROL 2005, my darling. That was eleven years ago.

MICHAEL Don't be stupid.

> **CAROL** *looks around the room and finds a recent newspaper. She shows it to him.*

CAROL Look at the date.

> **MICHAEL** *does so, in disbelief.*

…It's all right – you've got all those drugs pumping into you. It'll sort itself out.

MICHAEL I don't understand.

CAROL I'll find a doctor.

> **CAROL** *heads out of the door.*

MICHAEL Wait! *(she stops)* …Show me your hands…

> *She approaches* **MICHAEL** *and shows him her aging hands. As she does so, the lights fade to blackout.*

> *Authors Note: The dates and years should be adjusted in the above dialogue, depending on the year of the production.*

Scene Four

Lights rise on the hospital room, around noon, the same day. **CAROL** *is standing stage right.*

PAUL *is just inside the door at stage left.*

PAUL *(to* **MICHAEL***)* What is my name?

CAROL He's been told your –

PAUL *(putting his hand out to* **CAROL***)* Stop it. Let him answer.

MICHAEL It's Paul. They've told me that. But I don't know you.

PAUL The doctor spoke to me. It's difficult to know what to – I mean – I don't think they know what's going on either. It's unbelievable. This does happen sometimes when people come out of – ...They lose their speech, the personality changes, memory gets...lost... Look – it's okay. I mean – this is a temporary thing – in a few days, you'll – ...Just tell me – do you recognize me at all?

MICHAEL You were my nurse. I thought you were the nurse.

PAUL ...Look at me.

PAUL *goes over to the bed.*

...Look at me, Michael. It's me. *(he smiles at him)* ...It's me.

MICHAEL *looks to* **CAROL** *for help.*

CAROL This may not be the right time.

PAUL *(to* **CAROL***)* I don't care. How would *you* feel?

21

CAROL It's Michael's feelings I'm concerned about.

PAUL *(to* **MICHAEL***)* Remember me. Remember.

MICHAEL ...You're Paul?

PAUL Yes. Yes!

MICHAEL Hello, Paul.

PAUL *(yelling)* Damn it, Michael! It's me. For god's sake!

> **CAROL** *crosses the room quickly towards the door in order to call for help.*

Don't you dare, Carol.

CAROL I think we should –

PAUL Don't get anyone.

CAROL You're stressing him. And you've clearly not listened to the Doctor. I thought they explained.

PAUL Of course they explained. But I don't accept it. I just thought – I thought that when I was actually here... *(to* **MICHAEL** *again)* Michael – come on. Come on! It's Paul. Paul!

> *He touches* **MICHAEL***'s face and this makes him uncomfortable.*

MICHAEL Mum – get the – I need the –

> **CAROL** *exits immediately.*

(to **PAUL***)* I'm really sorry. And I don't know what's going on here. But you're making me very uncomfortable.

> **PAUL** *moves away.*

PAUL I'm sorry.

MICHAEL This is very odd. I'm trying to – ...I really just don't know you. Or I don't remember you. I've lost – I seem to have lost all this time.

PAUL I know. I can see. …All right. Look – erm, when you're better, suddenly it'll all come back. It's memory loss. It's temporary. I don't want you to worry about it. I'll wait. See how things are tomorrow. But it's hard, Michael – for me, I mean. You must understand that. I've been so frightened. All these weeks. And waited for you. Right here. I was right here. Waiting for you to wake up. And now you've opened your eyes and – you *can't* see me. You're not well. But you should know that we've been together for ten years. Ten years. The eleven years you seem not to remember right now – that was the time you were with me…more or less. Those ten or eleven years were *my* years. It wasn't perfect. But there were many, many wonderful times. You need to find them all, Michael. All those days you've lost. You must find it. And I'll help you do that. I'm your partner – and we always do things together.

CAROL *returns and* **PAUL** *stands up.*

…I'm going to pick up a few things. Some things to help you. Then I'll come straight back. Because this is where I belong, Michael. Don't forget that. *(to* **CAROL***)* Don't forget that.

PAUL *heads for the exit, pausing in the doorway.*

…I love you, Michael.

He exits. Fade to blackout.

Music plays –

Yesterday (McCARTNEY) – Sung by Matt Monro

Scene Five

Music fades out. Evening, a couple of days later. In a corner of the room there is a huge pile of newspapers, tied up in bundles. MICHAEL *is now more physically active and lights rise on* CAROL *helping him get out of the bed.*

There is a bottle of some kind of vitamin drink nearby on a table.

CAROL Are you sure you only want a piss?

MICHAEL Reasonably sure, yes. But you know how plans change.

CAROL I just think that if you're going to make all this effort...

MICHAEL I don't mind the effort. I'm thrilled that I can get out of this fucking bed.

CAROL Are you sure you don't need the nurse?

MICHAEL I'm not sure of anything. *(reacting to stiffness in his back)* Argh! ...Christ.

CAROL Press the button, get one of the nurses in here.

MICHAEL I'm all right. ...Let me go.

She lets him go and he does a long painful stretch to pull himself upright.

...Oh...! Well, here we are. Back on dry land.

CAROL Use your stick.

MICHAEL I don't need the –

CAROL Take the sticks.

She forces him to take hold of two walking sticks.

…The nurses have enough to do without worrying about picking *you* up off the floor. I'll help you to the lavatory.

MICHAEL I'm not ready yet. I just want to walk a bit and… *(looks around the room)* …take a look out the window.

MICHAEL *walks over to the window.*

CAROL Walk slowly. You're still fragile.

MICHAEL *(looking out the window)* …It's funny how everybody just behaves as though nothing happened.

CAROL Nothing did happen, not to them.

MICHAEL It must be terribly strange when you die – the thought that everything is going to carry on as normal. People at the supermarket, on buses, doing the ironing. The whole world carrying on in your absence. As though you didn't matter at all.

CAROL You're in a cheery mood.

MICHAEL Just making observations.

CAROL Yes – about death. …In a hospital. It's delightful.

MICHAEL *studies his reflection in the window.*

MICHAEL …It's still a shock – this face. So old. I have more hair than this. I do. And better skin. …What's happened in the last eleven years?

CAROL To you? Or to all of us?

MICHAEL Should I find out? Read all the newspapers? Think of all the television I've missed.

CAROL Don't worry, darling, I know it's been eleven whole years, but you haven't missed a thing. Just endless singing competitions and dancing competitions. It's like the God of Entertainment came down and threw

up over all of us. …You still don't remember anything
at all?

MICHAEL It's worse than that. I still don't believe anybody
in this building is telling me the truth.

CAROL They wouldn't lie to you. And I never would.

MICHAEL I know. You all just expect me to accept the
unbelievable?

CAROL In your own time. But we do, right now, expect you
to trust us.

MICHAEL How can somebody lose all that?

> **MICHAEL** *starts to move around the room.*

CAROL You didn't lose the days. You lived them. Every
second. It's only the memories you've lost. You were
here, Michael. You were here for all of it.

MICHAEL Then show me the evidence.

CAROL Of course we will. We'll help you piece it together.
So you can look back and then – move forward.

MICHAEL …Perhaps if I saw the paintings I've done. Could
you bring some in? Or take some photos?

CAROL I could, but you haven't really… I mean – you
stopped painting years ago.

MICHAEL I stopped? Why would I stop?

CAROL We all need to make a living, Michael. Paul felt
that – …I don't know. I wasn't exactly consulted about
it. But you took on the job at the insurance company
and there was never any time.

MICHAEL *(in disbelief)* I stopped painting!?

CAROL You made a choice. The choice all artists make.
Either paint – or eat.

MICHAEL That's incredible. I never *imagined* –

CAROL I was very sad about it – to be honest with you. I thought that your painting was – well, how can I put it – one of the best things about you. One of your special qualities. Most of us can't do anything. Artistically, I mean. I remember at school us having to draw either a horse or a house on stilts. Nobody was sure which one I'd done. And you can draw. You can paint. You're so lucky. And yet you don't.

MICHAEL I'm confused.

CAROL I thought your painting was wonderful. Not the kind of thing I'd have on my own wall. But nonetheless. You can still admire an artist but not their pictures. They were always so –

MICHAEL Surreal? Abstract?

CAROL Nonsensical. You know what I mean?

MICHAEL No.

CAROL But I loved that you painted. And if you painted something now, I'd cover every wall in my house. He should never have made you stop. Paul. He stamped on it. Spent an awful amount of energy persuading you it wasn't a good use of time, that nobody ever makes any money. Which is accurate – but not correct. He took the life out of you as far as I'm concerned.

MICHAEL Is that why you hate him?

CAROL I never said that I – …Well, yes it is. Amongst other things. I have to admit – though the circumstances are terrible – it's kind of gratifying that – *(she stops herself)*

MICHAEL Go on…

CAROL No, no. …Let's get you to the lavatory.

MICHAEL I can wait.

CAROL You haven't been for hours and you've had at least a litre of that awful vitamin drink. If you don't go soon, the dam is going to burst.

MICHAEL I'm going. – As soon as you finish the sentence.

CAROL …I was only saying that – and you mustn't say this to him – that amongst all the things you've forgotten… it's not necessarily a bad thing that you forgot about him.

MICHAEL He said he loved me. That he loves me.

CAROL I don't doubt that. In his way. But there's a lot of love in the world, Michael. I don't know that we need all of it. Some of it doesn't help us. If your father hadn't loved me, I think my life might have been better. …You remember your father?

MICHAEL Like it was yesterday.

CAROL Yes, I suppose it was just yesterday for you. About thirteen years, isn't it, more or less. Silly man. Anyway… here we are – in the hospital – and talking about death again. We're as crazy as each other.

MICHAEL I don't think the word 'crazy' was in my diagnosis.

CAROL Doesn't need diagnosis – it's in your genes. You can't do anything about it. (**MICHAEL** *looks at her*) …A little bit of crazy is very useful – in my experience. It helps you survive. …Michael, I know you feel you've lost so much through what has happened. But I do wonder if actually you're very lucky, in one respect. You have a chance to go back. Make a fresh start. A lot of people dream of doing that. But we're caught up – there are too many obstacles. But not for you – your pages are blank. I envy that.

She crosses to the door and opens it.

…Are we going?

MICHAEL *I'm* going. You're staying here.

CAROL You'll need help.

MICHAEL (*heading for the door*) I'll manage.

CAROL If you're grabbing on to the walking sticks, who's going to hold your penis?

MICHAEL *(stopped in his tracks)* The holding of my penis is my own concern! …You stay out of it. …I'm sure, if necessary, I'll find a volunteer. There never used to be a shortage of those…

MICHAEL exits the room. CAROL stands in the doorway watching his progress. Then she comes back into the room and looks for something to do. She sees the bottle of vitamin drink and pours herself some into a plastic cup. She drinks it, grimacing.

CAROL *(to herself)* If it tastes this bad, it must be good for you.

She crosses to the music player and hunts through the CD's and memory sticks to find something. One is unmarked, so she takes pot luck and puts that onto play.

Music is heard: The Requiem By Mozart

She looks puzzled but leaves it playing at a moderate volume. She then fetches one of her magazines and sits down to read. Shortly, PAUL enters, carrying a couple of shoe boxes and a small shoulder bag. He immediately sees MICHAEL is not there and looks to CAROL for an explanation.

He's taking a piss. …Providing he can find a nurse to, as it were, point him in the right direction.

PAUL Oh, okay. How is he today?

CAROL He's on his feet. Which has to be a good sign? Any time he's not horizontal can only be a positive.

PAUL Yes. I suppose.

He puts the boxes on the bed. He listens to the music for a moment.

…What is that music?

CAROL One of your friends sent it in. It's Mozart's Requiem. …Perhaps they thought he wasn't going to make it?

PAUL crosses to the player and turns it off.

Why have you – ? Michael likes Mozart.

PAUL I want to lighten the mood for when he gets back. I have a lot to talk to him about.

PAUL starts looking through the music.

…I need to find something that reminds him.

CAROL Of what?

PAUL Of us.

CAROL *(a short pause)* …I suppose it was you that organized all these.

She gestures to the bundles of newspapers.

PAUL Yes. They're weekly editions. Covering the whole of the missing period. It can only help. I couldn't get every single one of them, but most are there.

CAROL Must have been expensive.

PAUL No, actually. They were very helpful about that. I explained the circumstances, so they were generous. And rather fascinated. I suppose it is a very strange story. They suggested we sell the movie rights. I was left a bit speechless by that. *(he stops looking through the music)* And before you ask – yes, I did check with the Doctors first. About the newspapers. They agreed that it could be very useful… Not just to stimulate his memory, but to avoid conversations that might embarrass or confuse him. I mean there are things that have happened – major news events – that he just doesn't know about. They're not part of him. At least this way, he's informed. He's part of the conversation.

CAROL You do seem to have thought it all through. …Personally I avoid the news. If I happen to miss it completely for a week or two, I'm quite relieved. It's all so negative. Of course I'm sorry these terrible things happen to people, but I don't see how knowing about it helps *me* especially. Does the knowledge of someone else's death or tragedy help *me* live, helps me get through *my* day? Don't we all have enough struggles of our own without hearing about some murder in some town we've never heard of. Some chemical plant explosion. Is that useful to our own pursuit of happiness? I don't think so. I prefer the tennis. Or maybe that's just me.

PAUL Maybe it is.

CAROL Are you going to cut them open? We don't have any scissors. And I'm not using my teeth.

> **PAUL** *finds a dinner knife and uses this to cut the plastic tape around the bundles.*

…I might have a look at a few copies when I get bored. It's strange looking at the news in reverse. That happened once when I was cleaning out the loft. You find old magazines at the bottom of boxes, with pictures of these celebrities outside nightclubs. Full of life, all arrogance, shining teeth and Hugo Boss. And you think, "Oh dear… If only you knew what I know now". You see, you know what's coming to them. The car crash or drug overdose that's stalking them. It's very strange. You feel like God. …It's quite enjoyable. …I'll plunge in at random the next time he's asleep.

PAUL But keep them in order. Put the copy back into sequence. It's important that he starts with the last week he can remember – the first issue – and then works his way forward. It can't be jumbled. It has to be in sequence, brick by brick.

CAROL Those are your orders, are they?

PAUL Yes, they are.

Nothing said between them for a moment.

…Perhaps I'll get a drink.

CAROL Why don't you try some of that vile orange drink on the table. It makes you live longer – if it doesn't kill you.

PAUL No – I think it's better Michael has that. For the vitamins and everything. …He's walking about completely on his own, you said?

CAROL Yes – so it's working. You should have a glass.

PAUL I wasn't suggesting the drink was the thing that was –

CAROL I know, Paul. I was being sarcastic. Sorry you missed it. *(she goes back to reading her magazine)* …Next time I'll raise a flag.

PAUL I see you're in your usual shitty mood.

CAROL No, I'm fine. Not in the least bit 'shitty' *(a glance at the newspapers)* Especially now I've got so much reading to do.

PAUL Tell him – *(waiting till he gets her attention)* …Carol.

CAROL Yes?

PAUL Tell him I'm here and that I've just gone to get a coffee. I'll be back in five minutes.

CAROL *(changing subject)* …What's in the boxes?

PAUL Photographs. Some photographs.

CAROL *(putting down her magazine)* Oh yes?

PAUL Pictures of us together. Travel, birthdays, friends…

CAROL *gets up and wanders over to the boxes.*

CAROL …You think that's a good idea?

PAUL Why wouldn't it be?

CAROL Paul. Aren't you pushing him too hard? I mean, first there's all these newspapers and now on top of that, you're going to force feed him your holiday snaps. I think it's too much.

PAUL The sooner he remembers, the better.

CAROL The better for *you*, yes. But it may not be the right thing for Michael.

PAUL How could it possibly *not* be the right thing?

CAROL Look – you should let him remember in his own time. He doesn't even know who you are. And you're throwing all this history at him. I can see it being a problem for Michael. And I don't want him upset!

She picks up the boxes.

It would be much better if we save these for another day.

PAUL No – I'm not waiting. Give me the boxes.

CAROL I told you – it's not the right time for this. I won't let you.

PAUL *(strong, loud)* Carol – put them down!

CAROL Don't raise your voice to me.

PAUL This is to bring back the time we had together. Don't you want him to remember?

CAROL *takes the lid off one of the boxes and starts looking through.*

…Stop it! Those are private.

CAROL Private? He's my son!

PAUL Carol – give them to me.

CAROL No! It's not the right time.

> **PAUL** *crosses to her and grabs at the boxes, but* **CAROL**
> *refuses to let go. They look at each other – both taken*
> *aback that they are entering into a fight over these boxes.*
> *Then the struggle continues in earnest as they physically*
> *try to force the boxes away from each other. At the end,*
> *the boxes end up turned over, with the photos scattered*
> *onto the floor.*

PAUL Great! Just great!

CAROL Why aren't you listening to me? I am just trying
to –

PAUL *(very strong)* Shut up! For once, just shut up and sit
down!

> **CAROL** *retreats to the edge of the bed, where she sits.*

CAROL I find you very rude. And highly over-dramatic. You
people always are. It's incredibly grating.

> **PAUL** *goes onto his knees and starts picking up the*
> *photos and putting them back into the boxes.*

PAUL …When I'm here – from now on – I want you to
go somewhere else. You have your time with Michael.
And I'll have *my* time. Alone with him and without
interference. You understand? I don't want you here.
We'll have separate times.

CAROL I don't know if that suits me.

PAUL Then *make* it suit you.

CAROL I'm not changing my timetable, or restricting my
time with my son. So you just –

> **PAUL** *leaves the photographs and stares sternly at*
> **CAROL**.

PAUL I see you. You think I'm an idiot. But I see you.
I know exactly what you're up to.

CAROL Really?

PAUL You think you can wipe me out. Erase our time together. Well, you can't.

He shows her a handful of the photos.

Because he *will* remember. And when he does, he and I will carry on – whether you like it or not.

CAROL If he wants to.

PAUL Of course he wants to. We were very happy together.

CAROL *You* were happy. I'm not so sure about Michael.

PAUL Because you just don't know. You were always so ignorant about everything in his life.

CAROL Yes, I was kept very much in the dark. Until the days when he turned up at my house with his suitcase.

PAUL We resolved those problems. We resolved everything. In spite of you.

He finishes putting the photos back in the boxes.

…I want you to go now. I mean it. You need to get out.

CAROL *laughs.*

CAROL Oh I do like growing older. Nobody gets to tell you what to do anymore.

CAROL thinks for a moment and then lays down on the bed in a repeat of PAUL's similar action in scene one. PAUL stands – about to move back into battle – but at this moment, the door opens. MICHAEL is standing there.

MICHAEL Mission accomplished. *(seeing PAUL)* …Paul.

PAUL Hello, Michael.

MICHAEL They didn't tell me you were coming.

PAUL I come every day.

MICHAEL I know, I just meant – ...*(he sees* **CAROL** *laying on the bed)* ...Mother, I think that area's reserved for the unwell.

CAROL It's quite comfortable. I could lie here for ages.

MICHAEL Why don't you wander down the ward announcing that to all the patients. I'm sure they'll appreciate it.

CAROL Did you go?

MICHAEL Oh yes. Niagara Falls.

CAROL Did you need help?

MICHAEL I *did* as a matter of fact. It was quite a treat. And later he's bringing me coffee. I hear wedding bells. *(to* **PAUL***)* ...Oh, sorry. It's a – it's a joke. *(a pause)* ...Wrong joke I was just... ...Well, this is a little awkward, isn't it...

PAUL No, it's – ...It's all right.

MICHAEL *(seeing the boxes, excited)* Oh look – boxes! – Have you brought cakes?

PAUL No, I haven't brought cakes.

MICHAEL *(disappointed)* Oh. Then, I *won't* look forward to having one of those later.

He walks to the bed.

...Actually, I think I'll try the chair. But can we put it a bit more... I don't know, nearer the window?

PAUL *moves the armchair more downstage centre, and towards the window.*

PAUL Here?

MICHAEL Yes, thank you.

MICHAEL *sits in the armchair, looks out the window.* **CAROL** *sits up.*

…Yes, that's much better. …I'm quite taken with this view. It's the chaos of it. Beautiful trees by ugly concrete, children playing by ambulances. Sad people with flowers. Happy ones with suitcases. All in a jumble. Have you noticed? And at night there's very murky lighting. Old lights. Dirty, sickly, mustardy lights. Or maybe that's just the way it feels? This place needs colour. I thought I might paint something. Something big.

Looking around and seeing the huge blank wall behind his bed.

…On the wall, even? Yes, a giant mural. Am I allowed to paint on the wall? No, of course I can't. But I don't see how they can stop me. Besides, the room needs something radical. Clean and clinical is all very well, but it doesn't *encourage* anybody to wake up does it? It lacks life. The very thing we're supposed to be hanging on to. Am I rambling?

Both **PAUL** *and* **CAROL** *speak at the same time.*

CAROL / **PAUL**
   Yes. /   No.

MICHAEL Where are my paints? I'm going to need everything.

CAROL You're meant to be taking it easy.

MICHAEL I'm meant to be *alive*. Taking a piss can no longer be the highlight of my day. So, the paints – where are they?

PAUL To be honest, I'm not sure what we did with all of it.

MICHAEL Meaning?

PAUL Well, you gave so much of the stuff away.

MICHAEL Gave it away!? My painting materials? No, I'd never do that.

PAUL You did. About five years ago, or something like that. The thing was –

CAROL *(intervening)* You stopped painting, darling. We already had this conversation.

MICHAEL *(turning to* **PAUL***)* Can you fully explain to me why?

PAUL Well, you know, Michael, it wasn't – it wasn't really going anywhere. It took up so much time. So we did *other* things – we travelled, went to shows, restaurants. And you were always busy at work. We all have to earn a living.

MICHAEL And we all have to be creative. If we can.

PAUL This is probably a long conversation.

MICHAEL No, I think it's quite short. I paint.

PAUL But I think as you get older –

MICHAEL But I didn't get older. I got younger.

PAUL …I'm not the enemy here.

> **CAROL** *gets up and walks around the room to get a good view of the back wall.*

CAROL …We'll find your oils and brushes. Or get you new ones. *(her arms spread out to encompass the wall)* …What are you thinking?

MICHAEL *(turning to the wall)* Abstract. Surreal. Colour. Lots of colour. Something to frighten the cleaner. Vibrant. Hopeful. Full of life. I want to leave my mark here. After all, I'm a bit of a story, aren't I?

CAROL Yes, Paul wants to make a movie out of it.

PAUL That is not what I said.

CAROL Wasn't it? I wasn't really listening.

MICHAEL This is very exciting. I'll start tonight. Can you both get some paints tonight?

PAUL We'll have to check with everybody here first.

MICHAEL Oh to hell with them! What are they going to do? Confiscate my drip? This is Art – expression. It's what I've always done. – Until I stopped!

PAUL It was something we decided together.

MICHAEL Then I don't know who I was. I wasn't me anymore. Thank god I've woken up now.

CAROL I couldn't put it better myself.

PAUL *(agitated)* You don't understand! Things happen over time, circumstances change.

And what I did – what we did – was the best decision at that moment. You've forgotten.

CAROL Of course he's forgotten. You've not been paying attention at all, have you?

PAUL When we have time – I will explain it all. So much happened, so many years. You need to give me time to – take you through everything. When you start to remember – you'll realize – …you'll understand. Just trust me on that.

CAROL And while you're scrambling around for that trust, I'll go and buy the paints.

PAUL Will you shut up, Carol. Stop grabbing at each opportunity to –

CAROL You know, you've been telling me to 'shut up' quite a lot recently, it's getting very tiresome.

PAUL Pouncing on anything negative, anything you think might help to –

CAROL To what?

PAUL To push me out!

CAROL Oh really?

PAUL You won't win. You hear me? You will not win.

CAROL Let's see, shall we?

MICHAEL What's going on here?

CAROL Nothing important. You relax. Do you want a drink?

MICHAEL Yes, actually I do, but –

PAUL I'll get it.

> **CAROL** *and* **PAUL** *both go to the bottle of orange liquid and almost fight physically again over who is going to pour it.*

...I said – *I'll* get it.

CAROL I can manage!

> **CAROL** *pours a cup of the drink.*

PAUL ...You're not going to change who he is. Who he was. So don't try.

> **PAUL** *takes the drink from* **CAROL**'*s hands and takes it to* **MICHAEL**.

CAROL I just want – when he fully recovers – for Michael to be the best of himself. Not the worst of himself.

PAUL And that's me, is it? All the bad things?

CAROL I never said that exactly. Though you're driving up the right avenue.

PAUL What were you hoping for? For him to wake up straight?

MICHAEL Oh dear.

CAROL Straight? You think that's what all this is about?

PAUL I think that's the gist of it, yes.

MICHAEL *(calling out)* Nurse!

CAROL Michael, be quiet. Now listen to me, Paul. I don't dislike you because of your sexual preferences. Though it doesn't surprise me that you try and tie all that up in one neat parcel. And I don't blame you for making my son your lover. Yes, it's true he flirted in both directions before you came along and put your stamp on him. But I've known all about my son and his preferences for a long, long time. Mothers know. We spend almost every minute with our boys, watching them grow and form their view of the world. And we know. Much sooner than you think. We just don't talk about it. It's not necessary to, because the love never changes. It just adjusts. So don't think I somehow resent you having a relationship with my son, because you're very far from the truth on that one. I don't judge anyone based on their sexuality, skin colour, or whether they're fat, thin, foreign, or ginger. People are so ridiculous. They always seek a special reason for why they're disliked by others. When actually the reason they're disliked is so much simpler – they have a shit personality. And you've used yours to mould Michael into the person you want him to be. To bring him down to your own hugely uninteresting level. And it's not the person he was, nor the person *I* want him to be. The truth is, I liked my son better eleven years ago. He was a finer person, a better son, a more fascinating, colourful human being. And if this coma, this terrible thing, has brought him back to where he was before you came along – then I celebrate that. You covered over so much of what made him unique – you painted him beige. You may have loved him. Probably you still do. But you also ruined him. If you take a moment to remember how he was ten years ago, and how he was in the months before the accident. You'll see the difference. It makes me terribly sad. And the hardest thing of all is that I believe you know it. You see it too, as clearly as I do. That you stripped away all that was special about him. In order that the two of you could match up and get along. But up to this moment, you've just never admitted it. *(a short pause)* ...Tell me I'm wrong. ...Paul? Tell me – I'm wrong.

PAUL *says nothing.* **CAROL** *goes to get her handbag.*

...Well, if this conversation's over, I think I'll have a Mochaccino.

CAROL *exits from the room.*

PAUL   ...I don't know what to say. Your mother has the devil inside her.

MICHAEL That much I remember.

PAUL I need to go and talk to her. I need to – ...I'm sorry about all this. *(he heads for the door)* ...Do you need anything?

MICHAEL To be on my own.

PAUL *nods and exits.* **MICHAEL** *is now alone in the room. He lets out a deep breath. He gets up from the chair and stares out of the window. Then he looks at the pile of newspapers. He takes the first copy. He sits down on the edge of the bed with the newspaper.*

...All right. Let's make a start...

He opens the newspaper and begins to read. Lights dim slowly on **MICHAEL**. *As they do so –*

Music begins to play –

 Clocks By Coldplay *(Instrumental Version)*

Video sequence –

(stopping painting and cleaning his hands) I've always thought being naughty was underrated. ...We haven't seen you for a couple of days.

PAUL No.

MICHAEL Busy selling stuff?

PAUL The preferred term is 'marketing' – it's not only – *(giving up)* ...Yes, selling stuff.

MICHAEL Mum – are you going to say hello?

CAROL I don't think so.

PAUL We're still not speaking.

MICHAEL Oh, don't worry about that. She once didn't speak to me for three whole months. And that's tough when you're a six year old.

CAROL That's a lie.

MICHAEL I know, mum, I was only joking.

He mouths silently to **PAUL** *"I'm not joking".*

PAUL So how is everything? The test results okay?

MICHAEL They've tested absolutely everything, and today were able to officially confirm that I'm 'definitely alive'. Beyond that, I'm still a mystery. They've been experimenting a bit too. A parade of medical students have gawked at me as though I have flowers growing out of my head. The whole building finds me fascinating. They've even hypnotized me.

PAUL Really? How was that?

MICHAEL Don't know, I was hypnotized. You just zone out. But afterwards, you feel quite good. Like you had a nap on a warm afternoon – it's nice. And they tell you all the things you said. But I'm kind of convinced it was all clips from movies. All the things I remembered actually happened to James Stewart. I haven't told the hypnotist. I thought it might blow her confidence. Though I think she got suspicious when I mentioned the giant rabbit.

PAUL *laughs.*

PAUL But still nothing...? Nothing's coming back?

MICHAEL Nothing at all. As far as I'm concerned, right now – it's eleven years ago. Whatever the newspapers say.

PAUL But you're still recovering, so...

MICHAEL I know.

PAUL Can we sit for a minute? I need to tell you something.

They sit on the edge of the bed.

...I've been thinking a lot. I had it all planned out. The things to say, the steps to make in order to – help you, help both of us. And I felt I had a lot to explain – which I do. But I've decided that making excuses or finding reasons – that none of that has any point. I mean, what's done is done. You can't go back. The point I'm making is – ...that what Carol said – a few days ago... Well, I think – I think she might be right.

CAROL *looks up from her magazine.*

I've seen you painting the mural, seen how happy it makes you. And it reminds me of the man I first met, all those years ago. And I like him better. I think I took a lot away from him. From you. It's all my fault. I took a fascinating guy and – somehow – I made him plain, uninteresting. I turned you into me. And I'm genuinely sorry.

MICHAEL But you said we were happy together.

PAUL And I believed that. At the time. I resisted any suggestion that we weren't. But your mother really drove it home to me. She says terrible things. She lies. And when at her very worst – she tells the truth. I see now that it *is* the truth. I wish I'd realized earlier. Several years earlier, in fact. Things would have been better – between us. Somehow, despite all our arguments, the grayness of everything, I convinced myself all was fine. Not ever wonderful, we never reached those heights. It was always – complicated. And it's obvious to me now that I remembered it all differently to how it actually was. I'm just not sure any more if memory is a reliable thing. The replay is very different to the reality. I convinced myself we had this great relationship and this series of happy memories, but – as it happened, when it actually happened, I'm not certain it was ever really that good. …You know how people in America say they remember exactly what they were doing and where they were when Kennedy was assassinated? They now believe that half those people weren't in that place, were not doing what they thought. The mind just pieced something together for them. They *want* to remember how it was. But they actually don't and so something is gathered from other memories of the time, things they've read, things other people have said. The brain provides them with the memory they want. Even if it's false – a lie. And I think I can take apart every happy memory I have of us and see that I've manipulated it. In truth, it wasn't a good relationship. It was no more than reasonable companionship. And that's not enough. We deserve better. You especially. And you've been given a chance to forget about it all. You should take it. …So – I'm going to collect a few things. To make it easier for you to make a clean start.

PAUL *proceeds to gather up a few personal items from around the room. A card he wrote, the box of photographs, and a couple of individual framed pictures.*

MICHAEL You don't have to do this. At least leave the photos.

PAUL You don't even recognize these photos. The images aren't real for you. And the smiles aren't real for me.

MICHAEL Mum – you need to say something.

PAUL She wants to say "I told you so". Don't you, Carol? But as we're not speaking to each other, she's painted herself into a corner. *(looking at her and the mural)* …Literally, in fact.

MICHAEL Does this mean you're not even going to visit?

PAUL Of course I'll visit. We're friends. I really want us to be friends.

MICHAEL I'd like that. Come tomorrow, we'll work our way through all the chocolates.

PAUL Tomorrow, I can't. Actually I'm going to be away a few days. We have a conference about the campaign.

MICHAEL *Your* campaign?

PAUL Yes, the washing powder. The campaign is going nationwide.

MICHAEL That's great. Everybody needs washing powder. Your providing a public service.

PAUL It's just soap, Michael. Half the world is soap. All these powders, dishwasher tablets, body washes, window cleaners – it's all soap. Parceled up with lots of ribbons and bullshit. But they take it terribly seriously, people make millions. So you have to do your best.

MICHAEL And the campaign is…?

PAUL *St Paul's.* The Cathedral of washing powders.

He opens his arms wide as though the words are displayed on a giant banner.

…'Have faith in your powder'.

His hands drop, a brief pause.

…And suddenly I realize I've wasted my entire life.

MICHAEL No! I like it – it's clever.

PAUL It's clever, but it's not art.

He finishes collecting all the items.

…So, that's everything. It's all done.

MICHAEL Stay a while.

PAUL I'm on lunch break. I really just wanted to say those things and – leave you alone. I hope you'll be happy with this new start.

MICHAEL And you?

PAUL I'm sure I'll find someone else eventually. A lot of people in marketing are single. We have trouble selling ourselves. It's ironies like that – that make you want to jump off a tall building.

MICHAEL …You know – I never really understood why you would have picked me in the first place.

PAUL Picked you?

MICHAEL To be your partner – boyfriend. I mean, the truth is – I'm not that great. I have a lot of bad habits. I get obsessed by my work, whatever I'm painting. I eat the wrong things. I always put my foot in it. I'm so sarcastic sometimes that people instantly hate me after just one badly chosen sentence. Plus, I snore. My snoring is legendary amongst the nurses here. The head nurse has it as her ring tone. And last night, I farted so loudly that I woke myself up. That can't possibly make me marriage material, can it? Also – putting my bowels carefully to one side for the moment, I have this awful family with this strange nasty streak running through us. And not just the family we never speak to. The ones we love and care for are equally appalling.

I'm not rich. I'm self-obsessed. The ego is – on the larger side. My body is average at best. I've seen a lot of it recently – just hanging there. I should go to the gym. But I won't. And never did. Clearly. And I don't believe – that in any way I'm a great catch. I mean, I'm not miserable – I'm rather jolly. Which can be an attractive thing. Plus I think I'm reasonably interesting, reasonably charming. But not – anything special. You lay in bed for a few weeks, you think about this kind of stuff. So I just wondered why? Why you picked me? You've got a job, you're good looking. You're very generous, clever…kind. So why me? I'm not 'the cathedral of boyfriends'.

PAUL You're nicer than you think. …Though, actually, us getting together was a series of accidents. I'd just broken up with someone and – …We happened to be in this place at the same time and you made me laugh and – …Then a few weeks later there was some dinner and you were there again. I don't think we were that interested in each other, but – …It's odd, isn't it, how many relationships just sort of stumble into existence. It was hardly fireworks, Romeo and Juliet. But we grew to like each other. And when you had the accident, I realized how much you meant to me. But it was much too late.

PAUL *looks at the mural.*

…Does it have a title?

MICHAEL 4000 days.

PAUL It's a good title.

PAUL *gently kisses* MICHAEL *on the cheek.*

…Goodbye.

As he is about to leave, CAROL *speaks.*

CAROL Paul – …Thank you.

PAUL *turns back to look at* **CAROL**.

PAUL … Are you talking to *me*…?

PAUL *exits.*

Lights fade to blackout.

Music –

A Bad Goodbye (CLINT BLACK)

Scene Two

A day or two later. The mural has now grown across the wall. It is now almost complete.

CAROL *enters with a couple of bags of shopping. She crosses to the table and puts out the items she has brought – various types of biscuits, teas, sweets, plus vitamin supplements. Music fades out.* **MICHAEL** *is on the bed, resting. She unloads the snacks onto the table.*

CAROL Are you awake?

MICHAEL I am if you brought biscuits.

CAROL Yes. Wheat, sugar, stabilizers, additives – all the things that ruin your health. Plus vitamins so we can pretend it never happened... You're not painting?

MICHAEL I'm a bit exhausted. I felt dizzy.

CAROL Don't over do it. You were warned that –

MICHAEL I know, I know. But I can't stop. Painting makes my heart pound in my chest. I get so excited, like a little kid at Disneyland. They do still have Disneyland?

CAROL Yes, but it's all gone corporate now. Mickey and Minnie have their own team of lawyers.

MICHAEL It's just great to create. Why don't people see that? Making something out of nothing helps you breathe. I love to *breathe*. Life's wonderful, isn't it?

CAROL It can be, sometimes, yes.

MICHAEL Sometimes? That's a terrible thing to say. There are people starving, living in misery.

CAROL I know.

MICHAEL You should never say that.

CAROL I know.

She stands at the window and lights a cigarette.

MICHAEL Help yourself to a chocolate. Pick out a box. I've got tons of the stuff. I used to get flowers, but now word has got out that I can eat normally again – all hell has broken loose. Though a lot of it is 'sugar-free organic'. When the fuck did that happen...!?

CAROL It's all the rage.

MICHAEL It's scandalous. What biscuits did you bring?

CAROL Lemon, marmalade, shortbread. ...Sugar-free organic.

MICHAEL *(sarcastic)* Oh good, my favorite...

CAROL It took me ages to get in this morning. The traffic is terrible. Will they let you drive when you get out of here?

MICHAEL Yes, of course.

CAROL Well don't bother. Nothing moves. It would be better if we all went everywhere on roller skates.

MICHAEL Like *Starlight Express.*

CAROL You remember that show?

MICHAEL I do – unfortunately.

CAROL Before I forget – there's a reporter coming tomorrow from the local newspaper. They want to photograph the mural. She asked me what happened to you exactly – how *did* you end up in a coma. I said "I don't know, dear. Ask one of the doctors." She expected me to be able to break it all down for her medically. "We only know the basics" I said, "Accident.

Coma. Memory loss. *(pointing to the mural)* Vandalism".
That's all I know.

MICHAEL Don't you want to know more? Didn't you ask?

CAROL That man still makes no sense to me. The minute
they put on that white coat, they start talking gibberish.

MICHAEL It's not gibberish, it's very clear. I suffered a
Subdural Hematoma. You could have at least told the
journalist that. Caused by a minor head injury, which
I can't remember.

CAROL Well, I remembered the bit about you not
remembering...

MICHAEL Blood collects between the skull and the brain
and when a vessel in the subdural space is ruptured,
blood escapes and forms into clots which causes great
pressure –

CAROL But I don't really need to know that, do I?

MICHAEL The brain swells due to the injury, but there is no
room to expand because of the skull, and so there is a
rise in this pressure.

CAROL Michael –

MICHAEL Please pay attention. When this equals the
arterial pressure, the blood flow to the brain is affected
and this is where the real damage begins to be caused.

CAROL Where have you learned all this?

MICHAEL It happened to me. So I'm interested. Aren't you
interested?

CAROL It just seems...

MICHAEL The bleeding into the subdural space is highly
dangerous, resulting in death for up to 65% of
patients. In other words – it's not a picnic. And those
who survive can end up in a coma. Not a state of deep
sleep as people often presume, but actually a period

of prolonged unconsciousness. ...Shouldn't you be writing this down?

CAROL I can't write and smoke at the same time.

MICHAEL One man famously awoke with the inability to recognize objects. He mistook his wife for a hat. Fortunately, I don't have either a wife or a hat – so that problem was avoided.

CAROL I didn't realize you were so well informed. Now I suppose you can show off in front of the reporter?

MICHAEL Not sure I want to. Is he pretty?

CAROL It's a young woman. And she is, yes. ...And she has a hat...!

She throws the cigarette out of the window, targetting it at a stranger below.

MICHAEL It would be a good opportunity to get the mural properly photographed. Before they destroy it.

CAROL I discussed that with the Deputy Manager. Restoring the wall back to how it was is *our* responsibility, apparently. We can either paint it over ourselves – or otherwise it'll be a thousand pounds.

MICHAEL We should take the money...

CAROL No, Michael, to pay *them* to clean it.

MICHAEL I know. I was being humorous.

CAROL Are you sure? You've not been well.

MICHAEL They definitely won't keep it?

CAROL I'm trying. Perhaps if we get some attention in the newspapers, they'll change their minds. It's a real work of art. A symbol of life. It should stay here where it's most needed. And anyway – it's news. It's good news. And heaven knows that's gone out of fashion in a hurry.

MICHAEL I just want to leave something behind.

CAROL The important thing is that you get out. Whether you leave a trail behind you or not.

MICHAEL The doctor said leaving here might be difficult for me. The world has changed in my absence. Moved on. I might find it upsetting. Everyone I know will suddenly look older. Your friends, my friends.

CAROL No, my friends don't look older. They've all been stretched, enhanced, injected. They look like teenagers. Frankenstein's teenagers, but nonetheless.

MICHAEL Then that part should be easy.

CAROL Providing you don't look at them too closely. You have to just glance occasionally. It's very easy to get transfixed. And if they see the look of horror on your face, they get offended.

MICHAEL They can fill me in on all the gossip. Though I'm up to speed on the news.

CAROL You've looked through all of those papers?

MICHAEL Every single one. It's incredible the awful things that have happened. Makes you want to go back to bed.

CAROL Are you going to need a bed like that at home? One that lifts up electronically? You'll just need an ordinary bed, won't you?

MICHAEL When you say home – you mean – ?

CAROL My home. Obviously. You'll come and stay with me – to recuperate. Though don't think you'll be painting murals all over. I just put in parquet flooring.

MICHAEL But I have a home with Paul.

CAROL I know, we have to sort that out. Your Uncle Colin has a van. I don't want you to even set foot in there. You won't remember any of it. It could be very traumatic.

MICHAEL But it's years of my life. Our life. It seems unfair to Paul.

CAROL You'll be a stranger in a strange place. That can't be good therapy, can it?

MICHAEL I used to like seeing him. When he came every day. When I woke up, I thought I was single. And now I am again.

CAROL Not for long. You had plenty of boyfriends before Paul. And before then, girlfriends too.

MICHAEL Mother…

CAROL I'm stating a fact, not a preference.

MICHAEL Nobody was right for me. I didn't feel at home with any of them.

CAROL No, that's not true. What about the blonde one – Horst.

MICHAEL *(pulling a face)* You remember Horst!?

CAROL I liked Horst. He was Austrian wasn't he? Worked in a supermarket. What was wrong with him?

MICHAEL He was Austrian! He worked in a supermarket…! …His name was Horst…!

CAROL Well…plenty more fish in the sea.

MICHAEL If you have the right rod…

> **CAROL** *chuckles at this. Then goes over to the table and selects a box of chocolates.*

…The other ones are organic.

CAROL Fuck organic.

MICHAEL Mother! Not in front of the mural!

CAROL You need to finish your painting quickly, Michael. You do know that? They'll be letting you go very soon.

MICHAEL Should I be frightened?

CAROL Why not? A bit of fear is good for you. You're never more alive than when you're scared. But you won't be alone. That I promise you.

She sits next to **MICHAEL** *on the bed and offers him a chocolate.*

MICHAEL *(gesturing to the window)* What's it like out there?

CAROL It's the same. Only – slightly worse.

MICHAEL Well, that's something to look forward to…

They each eat a chocolate. Lights fade out.

Scene Three

A day or two later. The mural is now complete, except for one final vaguely rectangular shape at the top. This has been marked out but not yet filled in with colour.

Lights rise on **MICHAEL**. *He is staring out the window.* **PAUL** *enters with his work bag slung over his shoulder and with two take-away cups of hot chocolate.*

PAUL I brought hot chocolate.

MICHAEL Great! I've missed hot chocolate. And I've missed you too. …Those statements, of course, should have been the other way round. But I've had a blood clot.

He takes the drink.

…Do we hug or shake hands?

PAUL I suppose…

> **PAUL** *offers his hand and they shake. But somehow they both decide at the same time that this is not enough and they hug affectionately. They separate gently and smile at each other.*

MICHAEL Funny the things you miss.

He drinks his hot chocolate. **PAUL** *looks at the mural.*

PAUL It's very impressive.

MICHAEL Just one piece missing.

PAUL Then you better get on with it. You only have two days left. …How do you feel about that?

MICHAEL Optimistic. But I'm moving in with mum. So she'll soon put a stop to that.

PAUL I'll make sure you have all your things. But I'll get it all boxed up and sealed, so you can choose the moment when you take a look. I'll try and write the year on each box – the year I think you bought the things. If that'll help?

MICHAEL *(nodding)* I guess.

PAUL Is that why you called me?

MICHAEL Partly, but – ...I wanted to tell you about something.

PAUL Okay. Do I need to sit down for this?

> **PAUL** *sits. But* **MICHAEL** *stays on his feet.*

MICHAEL I had this, erm – yesterday, not under hypnosis or anything – when I was on my own, late at night. I had this little flash of – what felt like memory. And it seemed real. Though I can't be sure. So I wanted to ask you – Did we ever – was there a Chinese restaurant with, about four floors, and red walls? Not a smart place, kind of grubby, the waiters were rude or unhappy – or both. And there was a large window with a kind of dragon decoration and a yellow shirt.

PAUL A dragon in a yellow shirt?

MICHAEL No – the person I was with. Wearing a really disgusting yellow shirt. But a happy shirt. ...Was that you?

PAUL I don't really like Chinese. I've tried it, but, er... I don't remember a place like that. Or a yellow shirt. ...I don't think that was me. Some other 'friend' of yours – perhaps.

MICHAEL It may not be a real memory, just some image.

PAUL But if it is. If it *is* real – if it *is* a memory – that's wonderful. It could be a door opening. I'm disappointed I'm not the guy standing behind it. But it's great, Michael, it really is.

MICHAEL He might have just been a fellow frustrated artist? Or some friend, a gay friend, even? There's a lot of it about… But it's exciting. I'm – cautiously optimistic that maybe – that it might all come back.

PAUL Do you feel in yourself that – that everything's still in there somewhere?

MICHAEL Yeah, I think so. They say – the doctors – that if you do get it back, it's not a sudden thing. Not a sudden flood of all your memories returning. It's moments. Bit by bit. Not a flood but – but little drops. See what I did there? It was a water analogy.

PAUL Yes, very impressive.

MICHAEL I thought so too. …Anyway – I wanted to tell you.

PAUL I'm glad you did. That's great. You phone me the minute you remember anything else.

MICHAEL I will.

PAUL *gets up from the chair and wanders over to the window.*

PAUL …Bet you can't wait to see a different view. I hate this view. It's not what the world looks like…

Something suddenly occurs to **PAUL**.

…Wait a second – *(turning back to* **MICHAEL***)* The Chinese place. Was the stairway inside really dark? And with velvet carpeting on the walls?

MICHAEL Maybe… *(he shrugs)*

PAUL It was only that – there was this place – …I only remember going there once, it was so awful. One of those dirty restaurants where you get indigestion before you've eaten anything. It was years ago. Did I go with *you*? It may not be the same place. I just had this vague image…*(another sudden memory)* …Oh my god! The shirt! The yellow fucking shirt!

MICHAEL Yes?

PAUL I *had* a yellow fucking shirt! *Years* ago. With music notes all over it. It was a horrible shirt – you hated it. I can't even remember why I – …You were painting, your life was surrounded by all these bright gaudy colours and for some reason I went shopping and bought this shirt to show you – to show you that I liked colour. That I was into bold, bright splashes – and I looked like – like a children's birthday party. It was yellow and vulgar and I *never* wore it again. Because – it wasn't me. But I wanted you to see me differently. That's why we went to that Chinese. *You* liked it. So I went with you. So that you'd think I wasn't a stuck-up boring prick in a suit – which I am! I wore a disgusting yellow shirt. And we had a disgusting meal. And you remember this?

MICHAEL I think so.

PAUL You remember?

MICHAEL Yes. Yes!

PAUL …Why!? Why in God's name? Of all the things you could have – …It was *so* insignificant. A bad meal. A bad date. It wasn't a good experience. Nobody who ate there *ever* had a good experience. And at that point – and this is the really bizarre thing – we weren't getting along. Not at all. We were stumbling. Falling at every hurdle. It was – instantly forgettable.

MICHAEL It's just the first drop.

PAUL Oh, I hope so, Michael. Oh my god – that would be so wonderful. …But of all the drops…! We've been to the Taj Mahal, swam in the ocean, made love on the riverbank. But a crappy yellow shirt and Kung Pao chicken? Jesus! It makes no sense. Why would you remember that?

MICHAEL *(laughing)* I don't know! I just think – I remember this vague feeling while I was there – that we were both trying so hard. It's the feeling I remember. The images are decoration. All I know is – that it meant something. It must have.

PAUL We could go back there. See if you remember more. I'll talk to Doctor Medina about it. We should – your first evening out of here – we'll go back there.

MICHAEL Have a meal?

PAUL Well, let's not be crazy. We're only just getting you *out* of hospital. But – to see those images for real. Maybe that's the key. Have you remembered anything else at all?

MICHAEL No. Just that one thing. ...Do you still have the yellow shirt, hidden in a bottom drawer somewhere?

PAUL No, of course not. It went straight in the bin the next day.

MICHAEL Then find something else with colour. And we'll go and spend some time at that place. ...Get to know each other.

PAUL ...Again...

MICHAEL I suppose.

PAUL Yes, I'd like that. ...But your mother won't. She talks to me now, but she still hates me.

MICHAEL Give her time. She hates most men. You shouldn't take it so personally. She's had three husbands and she resents *all* of them. Especially the ones that *died* on her. She finds that kind of behavior unforgiveable.

PAUL She never talks about them.

MICHAEL Buy her a whisky and a steak one day and she'll tell you everything. None of them ended happily. So she doesn't trust husbands and boyfriends. Not hers, nor mine. Unless, it turns out, they're fucking Austrian. In which case, she can't get me down the aisle fast enough. ...Of course – I don't know what she's been up to herself in this missing period.

PAUL You should ask her.

MICHAEL I don't need to – there's not been anybody. You can see it in her eyes.

PAUL She's not necessarily finished yet. There's still time. That goes for all of us. *(thinks for a moment)* Here – you should take these.

He gets a pen and a block of post-it notes (self adhesive paper notes) from his shoulder bag.

Post-it notes. Write down "yellow shirt – Chinese restaurant"

MICHAEL *takes a pen and writes as instructed.*

...And we'll put it on the wall. Each time you think of something – a memory or something that you *think* might be a memory, even if it's actually a scene from *It's a Wonderful Life* – write it down and put it up here.

PAUL *sticks the note somewhere on a side wall or on the door.*

MICHAEL Don't you have to take these to work?

PAUL We use them whenever we have an original idea. So I rarely need them. When I come back tomorrow, you can read them all out to me.

MICHAEL I can't promise anything. Besides, I have packing to do. Do I have any suitcases?

PAUL Your mum is arranging all that. And she'll have your room ready for you at her house, complete with a bottle of champagne I'll be sending over. So you can toast finally getting out of here.

MICHAEL That's very extravagant of you.

PAUL It's because of Daniel and Jonathan – whenever I see champagne on a shelf, I always think of those two and feel compelled to buy it. We went to Italy with them. I don't think they drank anything else the whole week.

MICHAEL *shrugs, not remembering them.*

…You'll like them. They're very quiet, very sweet. Very much in love. They sent you flowers – several bunches.

MICHAEL You should introduce me.

PAUL I will. Anyway – Daniel and Jonathan do this wonderful thing as a ritual every evening at home. After dinner, they have a glass of champagne together. A glass of champagne 'to celebrate the day'.

MICHAEL That *is* sweet. But what if the day has gone really, really badly?

PAUL Then they finish the bottle…!

MICHAEL *(laughing)* I like that. I'm going to do that. We should all do that. *(thinks for a moment)* …Italy?

He looks quizically at **PAUL**.

PAUL …What is it?

MICHAEL *says nothing. A moment later, he grabs the pen and the block of post-it notes and writes something down. He sticks it to the wall next to the other note.*

MICHAEL Italy. We bought a big carnival mask – to hang on the wall. A unicorn?

PAUL Yes!

MICHAEL *thinks of something else and writes another note and also sticks this to the wall.*

MICHAEL …Jonathan…

And another note.

…Driving by a lake. …Drinking in the sunshine…

And another.

…Tiramisu…

And another. And another. And another. Writing things down and sticking them on the wall in a frenzy.

PAUL What are you remembering?

MICHAEL *stops, turning to* **PAUL**, *full of emotion.*

MICHAEL …Everything.

PAUL *(excited)* Michael…!

MICHAEL Wait. No. Not everything. Not everything. *(he smiles)* …Only everything *good.*

He goes back to frenziedly writing and sticking the notes. **PAUL**, *amazed, sits down and watches.*

Music begins –

A reprise of: Remember (NILSSON)

Lights fade to blackout. The video screen descends into view.

Video sequence –

A series of video clips and photographic images on the screen. The footage covers the last eleven years of news items – world events, local events, celebrities, etc. But this time, all the news is positive. Joyful events, celebrations, artistic achievements, things that have made the world smile. The video plays with audio included on some of the clips. The sequence lasts for approximately two minutes.

When the video sequence ends, the screen disappears.

Scene Four

Two days later. The mural is now complete, with the final rectangular shape at the top painted yellow.

All of the other walls in the room are completely covered in bits of paper. Hundreds of post-it notes, but also things scribbled on the back of medical records, envelopes, random bits of paper, tissues, etc. Anything that can hold words.

MICHAEL's clothing and personal items have been packed into two suitcases that sit on the floor, still open. All the flowers and chocolates have been taken from the room.

CAROL enters. The music fades out.

CAROL I feel like Santa Claus.

MICHAEL follows her into the room. He is now dressed in normal clothes, ready to go home. The clothes are quite loose and baggy on him.

MICHAEL I enjoyed giving the flowers away to all the nurses. But when we started giving away the chocolates, I thought I was going to have a heart attack.

CAROL You couldn't have eaten them all.

MICHAEL I could have tried! I've lost so much weight while I've been in here.

CAROL That's a good thing.

MICHAEL It's a *terrible* thing. Eating is one of the world's great pleasures. I've got so much catching up to do.

CAROL People should eat healthily. The nurses are very insistent about that.

MICHAEL These are the same nurses currently working their way through seventeen boxes of Belgian truffles?

CAROL Yes. And they appreciate it – and now we've a lot less to carry home. I've only got a small car. So what next? We need to take down all those notes.

MICHAEL I'll find a box. I need to keep them all, just in case.

CAROL Michael, you're not going to forget everything again.

MICHAEL I'm not taking that chance. I'll do it. You have a break.

MICHAEL starts to remove the notes one by one and gather them in to some kind of empty box left over from a gift. As he does this, CAROL takes a photo of the mural with her mobile phone.

…We've got dozens of photos already.

CAROL Yes, but this one's just for me. …Have you decided yet if you're going back to work?

MICHAEL No. I'm not going.

CAROL Good. That's the right thing to do. …Just make *good* decisions about everything. I rarely managed that in my life. Hardly ever now I think about it. It's a terrible thing. We each make dozens of decisions every single day. But make three really bad ones and you can fuck up your entire life. So I want you to promise to be incredibly careful about all the paths you take. That's something I demand of you.

MICHAEL I promise.

CAROL sits down in the armchair.

...And you? What are *you* going to do when you get out of here?

CAROL Cook you a huge dinner. And at the weekend, we'll go for a long drive. Where shall we go?

MICHAEL I don't suppose you mind so long as we avoid the question.

CAROL I answered the question!

MICHAEL *(repeating)* What are *you* going to do – when you get out of here? With your life?

CAROL What I always do.

MICHAEL And that's enough?

CAROL I'm a divorcee, a widow, and an abandoned woman. In that order. It's a small club and nobody wants to be a member. I have no companion. I don't work. I'm not young. And my feet ache. What do you want me to do? Take up wind-surfing with the boy next door?

MICHAEL He was cute, the boy next door.

CAROL *That* you remember! Hands off – I'm saving him for a rainy day.

MICHAEL See – you're not done yet.

CAROL People do like to say that, don't they. "Oh there's a good few years left in you". But the truth is, I don't have strong desires to do anything anymore. The entire focus of my day is on being comfortable. A comfortable sofa, comfortable shoes, simple pleasures, an easy routine. I used to dream of playing tennis, walking in the mountains, riding in a speedboat. But now I just want a good pair of slippers and a decent film on TV.

MICHAEL Oh, stop that. I know a lot of very old people who are very young.

CAROL And I know a lot of very old people who thank god all that youthful vigor is over and done with. There's a lot of pleasure in not running about like headless chickens anymore. You finally throw the towel in, let all your breath out, and sink slowly into the cushions. Realizing you're old and passed-it can be such a relief. It's like telling the world to go stuff itself and then taking a nice warm bath.

MICHAEL In which you slowly drown... We have to find you somebody. Put a fire back in your belly.

CAROL Nonsense. I have *you*. I don't need anyone else.

At this moment, the door opens. **PAUL** *enters.*

With a big smile, he unzips and removes his jacket – to reveal that he is wearing an extremely gaudy bright yellow shirt. He presents it proudly.

...I should have brought my sunglasses.

PAUL Isn't it horrible!? I was so excited when I found it in the charity shop. *(to* **MICHAEL***)* It's not much like the original yellow shirt, of course, but it does have the same flavour of absolute desperation. Don't you think?

MICHAEL *(smiling)* It's disgusting.

PAUL *throws his jacket on to the bed.*

PAUL I knew you'd like it. And that this would be a very strange day for you. So, I wanted to do something that might make you smile. *(looking around)* ...Oh god, I am so thrilled that I never have to walk into this room again. I want to run out of here fast – never look back. *(to* **CAROL***)* Don't you feel the same?

CAROL I can't run – not with *my* feet.

PAUL But you understand what I'm saying?

CAROL Not usually, no.

PAUL Well, that's your loss. *(to* **MICHAEL***)* The packing – how are we getting on?

MICHAEL All but the last two pieces.

He collects the final two notes from the wall and puts them in the box.

PAUL Where are all the chocolates?

MICHAEL Don't mention that! I'll start crying.

MICHAEL *puts the box of notes into one of the suitcases.*

PAUL …Do we have to be officially released – or do we just go?

MICHAEL Doctor's already been in. Signed the paperwork, wished me luck, and headed off back down the ward. Another coma patient came in yesterday. Can you believe that? It never stops.

PAUL I know. This can be a terrible place. Which is why I can't wait for us all to go.

PAUL *shuts and locks the cases.*

…There's a journalist waiting for you downstairs. They had a really good response to the article, so they want to get a shot of you leaving the hospital. Not much good news ever comes out of here. So, like the mural, you're the current symbol of hope.

CAROL I'd love your French teacher to read that in the morning. He said in your school report that you had 'no hope whatsoever'. It'll make him choke on his cornflakes.

MICHAEL Why do you even remember that?

CAROL My head has a special vault for things that make me angry. It never empties. They shouldn't pre-judge people. There's plenty of time to change. …Unless of course, you can't be bothered.

CAROL *gets up and crosses to the suitcases.*

(to **PAUL***)* …Shall we take one each?

PAUL It's all right – I can manage both. *(to* **MICHAEL***)* So – do you want to go now – or…?

MICHAEL I'm not sure. I'm really not sure…

PAUL Michael – one step at a time. Go to your mums. Sleep. And then tomorrow, like the rest of us, you wait and see what happens. That's all you can do. *(to* **CAROL***)* …I'll wait by the car. *(to himself)* But first, I need to…

PAUL *goes over to the mural. He places his hand and rests his head gently on the wall, saying goodbye. Then he returns to the suitcases, picks both of them up, and with a smile of relief, he exits.*

CAROL *(a look at her watch)* …All right. So come on now, Michael. Let's be brave about this.

MICHAEL *is looking at the mural.*

…You can always paint another one. And I expect they'll need to get this room ready for somebody else. Which is a terrible thought, but – …But this is a happy day. For all of *us* anyway. So let's just step into the sunshine. *(***MICHAEL** *is now looking over at the door)* …Besides, that journalist is waiting. …Michael? *(he doesn't move)* …Michael – aren't you coming?

MICHAEL *(turning to* **CAROL***)* No. …No, Mum. …I'm going *home*…

MICHAEL *picks up* **PAUL***'s jacket and holds it close to him.*

CAROL Wait… Wait now, Michael. We talked about this.

MICHAEL It's only a second chance if you take it.

CAROL A second chance to what? To fail? To give up again on everything you love?

MICHAEL It'll be different this time.

CAROL You don't know that. He hasn't even said he's interested. He freely admits you made a terrible couple – that's why he let you go.

MICHAEL It just feels like too many memories to – to throw away.

CAROL We all have to do that. Life *makes* you do that. Sometimes it's the only way to survive.

MICHAEL I won't let go of them. Not me. Never again.

CAROL But Michael –

MICHAEL I'm sorry. This is how it has to be.

CAROL But what about – *(her heart breaking)* …But what about *me*…?

MICHAEL …You'll be fine.

CAROL I'll be *alone*.

MICHAEL *(a moment)* …Mum, we won't forget you.

CAROL I'd love that to be true. But it isn't, is it? The mothers always get left behind. …But you were mine again for a little while there, weren't you? Just a little while…

MICHAEL Come and visit at the weekend.

CAROL No, I can't do that. I have plans to be tired this weekend.

MICHAEL *(lost for words)* …What do you want me to say?

CAROL That you're certain it's the right decision. That it's a *good* decision…

MICHAEL *shrugs, not really knowing if it is or not.*

MICHAEL I'm awake. That's all I know.

He crosses to **CAROL** *and kisses her. He then walks to the door and exits.*

CAROL *is alone in the room. She feels suddenly lost and stands motionless, staring at the door.*

After a moment, a hospital worker enters the room (a role played by one of the Stage Management Team or an under-study). **CAROL** *does not react to him. He carries a pot of beige paint, a paint roller and tray.*

The hospital worker sets himself up in front of the mural, wets the roller in the tray of paint, and proceeds to paint over the mural, erasing it stroke by stroke.

As he begins to do this, music gently fades in –

Clocks – By Coldplay *(Instrumental)*

The lights very slowly fade to blackout.

The End

The music continues during the final curtain calls and as the audience leaves.

Act One

Property List

Large bunch of fresh flowers (p1)
A vase (p1)
A book (p1)
Fresh flowers, a smaller bunch, plus some sandwiches in a brown paper bag (p1)
A cigarette (p2)
A card (p2)
A packet of sandwiches (p3)
Paul – looks at his watch (p10)
Carol – looks at her watch (p10)
Drinking a cup of water (p13)
Cup of coffee and a bar of chocolate from a vending machine (p13)
Carol locates a photo of Paul and Michael together which has been placed by the window with various other portraits of family and friends (p18)
A recent newspaper (p20)
In a corner of the room there is a huge pile of newspapers, tied up in bundles (p24)
There is a bottle of some kind of vitamin drink nearby on a table (p24)
Two walking sticks (p25)
She sees the bottle of vitamin drink and pours herself some into a plastic cup (p29)
CD's and memory sticks (p29)
Magazines (p29)
Couple of shoe boxes and a small shoulder bag (p29)
Paul finds a dinner knife and uses this to cut the plastic tape around the bundles (p31)
The boxes end up turned over, with the photos scattered onto the floor (p34)
Handbag (p42)

Costume:
Paul – He is wearing his underclothes, plus is covered in a blanket or dressing gown (p12)

Lighting

Lights slowly rise on the hospital room (p1)
The lights fade to blackout (p11)
Lights rise dimly on the room. It is night time (p12)
The lights fade again to blackout (p12)
Lights rise on the hospital room (p13)
Lights fade to blackout (p20)
Lights rise on the hospital room, around noon (p21)
Fade to blackout (p23)
Lights rise (p24)
Lights dim slowly on Michael (p42)
When the video sequence ends, the music fades and we go to blackout (p43)

Sound/Effects

MUSIC "REMEMBER" (NILSSON) – Sung by Harry Nilsson (p1)

The music cross-fades from the auditorium to the music player onstage. Paul turns the music off (p1)

Paul turns on the music player with a nearby remote control. It plays:

"IN THE WEE SMALL HOURS OF THE MORNING" (MANN/HILLARD) – Sung by Frank Sinatra (p11)
The music cross-fades from the player to the auditorium (p11)

The music continues (p12)

A red flashing light in the room (p12)

The music ends (p13)

She presses a button and the top end of the bed electronically raises so Michael is sitting uprights (p14)

Music plays – "YESTERDAY" (McCARTNEY) – Sung by Matt Monro (p23)

Music fades out (p24)

Music is heard: "THE REQUIEM" – by Mozart….playing at a moderate volume (p29)

Paul crosses to the player and turns it off (p30)

Music begins to play – "CLOCKS" – by Coldplay (Instrumental version) (p43)

Video sequence – A series of video clips and photographic images start to be displayed or projected on a video screen that descends into view. The footage covers the last eleven years of news items – world events, local events, celebrity scandals, etc., etc. The video plays with audio included on some of the clips. All of the clips are of dramatic and serious events. The sequence lasts for approximately 2 minutes (p43)

Act Two

Property List

The bundle of newspapers has disappeared, now only a few copies remain. The room is full of artistic painting materials. A table is piled high with boxes of chocolates and other gifts. A lot of the medical equipment has been removed from the room (p44)

Paul proceeds to gather up a few personal items from around the room. A card he wrote, the box of photographs, and a couple of individual framed pictures (p47)

Carol enters with a couple of bags of shopping. She crosses to